What is Supply and Demand?

Gare
Thompson

Crabtree Publishing Company

www.crabtreebooks.com

Crabtree Publishing Company

www.crabtreebooks.com

Author: Gare Thompson
Publishing plan research and development:
   Sean Charlebois, Reagan Miller
   Crabtree Publishing Company
Coordinating editor: Chester Fisher
Series editor: Gare Thompson Associates
Editor: Molly Aloian
Proofreader: Crystal Sikkens
Editorial director: Kathy Middleton
Production coordinator: Margaret Salter
Prepress technician: Margaret Salter
Project manager: Kumar Kunal (Q2AMEDIA)
Art direction: Harleen Mehta (Q2AMEDIA)
Cover design: Shruti Aggarwal (Q2AMEDIA)
Design: Shruti Aggarwal (Q2AMEDIA)
Photo research: Ekta Sharma (Q2AMEDIA)

Photographs:
American Honda Motor Co Inc: p. 23 (top), 26 (bottom)
Corbis: Bettmann: p. 25 (bottom); K.M. Westermann: p. 27;
   Ariel Skelley: p. 29
Dreamstime: Colleen Coombe: p. 8 (middle); Madmaxer: p. 8
   (bottom)
Fotolia: Beboy: p. 17
Istockphoto: Andrew Penner: p. 7; William Murphy: p. 14;
   Werner Stoffberg: p. 26 (top)
Masterfile: p. 6
Photolibrary: Leber Gerhard: p. 4; Imagesource: p. 5; Hirb: p. 11 (top);
   Superstock Inc: p. 13; Boutet Jean-Pierrre: p. 18; Bruce Yuan-Yue
   Bi/Lonely Planet Images: p. 19; Lutz Pape: cover
Q2AMedia Art Bank: p. 10, 12, 24
Reuters: Issei Kato: p. 16; Larry Downing: p. 28
Shutterstock: p. 9, 21 (bottom); Iofoto: p. 11 (bottom); Hanna
   Monika: p. 15; Abutyrin: p. 20; Lisa F. Young: title page, p. 21
   (top); WizData Inc: p. 22; Paul Paladin: p. 23 (bottom); Alexei
   Novikov: p. 25 (top); Hvoya: cover

Library and Archives Canada Cataloguing in Publication
Thompson, Gare
      What is supply and demand? / Gare Thompson.

(Economics in action)
Includes index.
ISBN 978-0-7787-4446-7 (bound).--ISBN 978-0-7787-4457-3 (pbk.)

      1. Supply and demand--Juvenile literature. I. Title.
II. Series: Economics in action (St. Catherines, Ont.)

HB801.T46 2010   j338.5'21   C2009-906268-2

Library of Congress Cataloging-in-Publication Data

Thompson, Gare.
 What is supply and demand? / Gare Thompson.
      p. cm. -- (Economics in action)
 Includes index.
 ISBN 978-0-7787-4457-3 (pbk. : alk. paper) -- ISBN 978-0-7787-4446-7
(reinforced library binding : alk. paper)
 1. Supply and demand--Juvenile literature. I. Title. II. Series.

 HB801.T528 2009
 338.5'21--dc22

                                            2009042777

Crabtree Publishing Company

www.crabtreebooks.com   1-800-387-7650

Printed in the USA/122009/BG20091103

Published in Canada
Crabtree Publishing
616 Welland Ave.
St. Catharines, ON
L2M 5V6

Published in the United States
Crabtree Publishing
PMB 59051
350 Fifth Avenue, 59th Floor
New York, New York 10118

Published in the United Kingdom
Crabtree Publishing
Maritime House
Basin Road North, Hove
BN41 1WR

Published in Australia
Crabtree Publishing
386 Mt. Alexander Rd.
Ascot Vale (Melbourne)
VIC 3032

Contents

What is Supply and Demand?   4

Needs and Wants   8

Prices: The Law of Demand   10

Prices and Quantity: The Law of Supply   12

The Role of Competition   16

Big Picture: The Global Market   20

Things Change   22

Finding a Balance   24

The Government Steps In   28

Glossary   30

Index and Webfinder   32

What is Supply and Demand?

Two simple words are at the heart of economics. Those words are **supply** and **demand**. You probably have heard the words before, but do they really affect you? You bet they do. You are a **consumer**. You spend money when you buy **goods** and **services**.

Goods are products, such as sneakers, DVDs, and clothes. Services are the actions or activities that people provide for others, such as teaching or driving a bus. As a consumer, you help determine which products are made, the **quantity** that is produced, and the price at which the products are sold. You also help determine which services people offer and how much they charge. That's what supply and demand is all about.

But what exactly do these terms MEAN?

• Supply is the quantity of resources, goods, or services that sellers offer at various prices at a particular time.

• Demand is the number of consumers willing and able to purchase a good or service at a given price.

• Quantity is the amount of goods or services that is produced or purchased.

▼ Games are popular goods with consumers.

Think of it this way. A new game for the Xbox 360 is going on sale this Saturday. You have read that there will only be a limited quantity available. You want to make sure you get a copy before the store is sold out. Finally, the big day arrives. You go to the store early in the morning. There already is a long line. Along with several dozen other hardcore gamers, you run through the doors the minute the store opens to purchase the game. The sales clerk happily takes your money. The game is yours! Mission accomplished. You are one satisfied consumer.

How did your actions relate to supply and demand?

• You were the consumer, willing and able to purchase the goods (the game) at a given price.

• You wanted to buy the game; that is demand.

• The seller (the store) was willing to make a quantity of goods (the game) available at a particular time.

Who's Who in Supply and Demand
You the consumer just experienced supply and demand at work. The consumer plays an important role in supply and demand, but there are other participants, as well. Someone made the goods you bought and someone sold the goods to the store. A producer **manufactures** the product. In this case, the producer is the factory that made the game you bought. Another participant in supply and demand is the distributor. The distributor sells the product to stores and businesses. In the case of the game, the distributor was the salesperson who sold the game to the store. The distributor buys from the producer and sells to the store.

◄ Adults over 18 now make up almost half of all game players.

▲ Kids as consumers influence what toys are made.

So which role do you play? Well, most often you are the consumer. Consumers have power. All the participants in the supply and demand chain want your business. They will work hard to win your support. The decisions you make as a consumer affect the producer, distributor, and seller.

Consumers can increase or decrease sales of products. These increases and decreases affect supply and demand. The way you spend your money affects the **economy**. Let's look at how an economy works.

Point of Information

Teens are a powerful consumer force. In the U.S. market, 12-to-17-year-olds spent about $112.5 billion in 2003. That's a lot of power and makes producers of goods and services listen to what teens want!

Free Market Economy

An economy is how a country manages its money, goods and services, and resources. Supply and demand work best in a specific kind of economy, called a **free market economy**. What do Brazil, the United States, China, Canada, Mexico, Japan, and Russia all have in common? They all have a free market economy. That means that each country buys and sells things without interference from outside sources. In other words, no one tells them what to sell, how to price it, and how much they can sell.

For example, Canada sells oil. The government does not tell the oil producers at what price to sell the oil, how much oil they can sell, or how to sell it. The oil producers make all those decisions based on their supply and the demand for oil. Supply and demand is the main force in a free market economy. So let's look at how supply and demand works.

▼ Canada sells oil to many countries. It has a free market economy.

Needs and Wants

So who decides which goods and services will be offered? Well, you as the consumer, have a great influence. You determine what's offered through your demands. Your demands are based on your needs and wants.

What Do You Need?

Needs are things essential to life, such as food, clothes, and medical care. Needs are things that allow you to survive and that you can't do without. Since all people have these basic needs, they create a demand in the market. For example, you need food to live. Without it you would starve. Clothes are a need, too. People who live in cold areas need warm clothes to live. So, in colder regions people create a demand for warm clothes.

▲ Housing is a need.

▲ An expensive television is a want.

What Do You Want?

You also have wants. Wants are things you can live without but want to buy anyway. Wants include luxury items, such as designer clothes expensive electronics, and **intangible** things, such as taking a trip or going to the movies. Wants often make you feel better.

Here's how a consumer creates demand. Imagine that you are wearing the latest athletic shoes. Those shoes look great, and your friends envy them and want to get a pair for themselves. Suppliers of these shoes recognize this want. So they supply the goods to satisfy it. They produce many different types of athletic shoe—for casual wear, for sports— even for special occasions! They change the design often so people will always want the "latest" shoe.

Choices, Choices

Few consumers can buy everything they want or need. No one's income or spending money is unlimited. Therefore, all consumers make choices. They decide how, when, and where to use their money. Their choices help determine what goods and services are produced.

Suppliers try to influence these choices. One way they do this is through **advertising**. Ads promote a particular product. Ads tell consumers all about the benefits of the products and why people need the products. Ads help sell a product by creating a perceived need: the ad makes consumers think they must have the product!

Ads for **hybrid** cars are a good example of how advertising influences consumers. These ads suggest that owning a hybrid car is a good way to "save the planet." The ads say that hybrids use less gas so they pollute less. Manufacturers of hybrid cars create ads to appeal to people who want to protect the environment and use less energy. They hope their ads will influence people to buy hybrid cars. Do you think their ads will work? What would you do?

▲ This customer is creating demand by wanting the "latest" shoe.

Point of Information

Some people run marathons, or long-distance races, barefoot. Companies are now making a sneaker that is very thin and fits the foot like a glove. Would you want this new sneaker?

Prices: The Law of Demand

In addition to needs and wants, one other thing determines what consumers will buy: price. But how are prices determined?

You know there are laws in science. Well, there are also laws in economics. The laws in economics govern the way things work in the marketplace, including how goods and services are priced. Let's look at the **law of demand**.

The law of demand states that

- if the price of a good goes up, people buy less of it, if all other things are equal;

- if the price of a good goes down, people buy more of it, if all other things are equal. Consumers buy more of a product at a lower price, and buy it more often, than they do at a higher price.

The Law of Demand at Work

Here's how the law works. Let's say that the price of CDs decreases. However, the price of song downloads remains the same. The price of song downloads is now higher than that of CDs. Consumers notice the difference in price and make choices.

▶ This graph shows the law of demand. If the price goes up, people buy less. If the price goes down, people buy more.

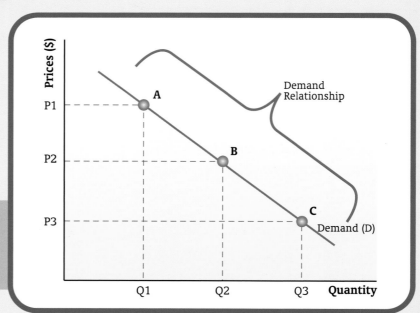

Many people buy more CDs as their price drops. Why? They think CDs are a better bargain and a smarter purchase. They think they are getting more for their money. The demand for CDs has increased.

Then the price of CDs goes up. So now people buy fewer CDs. They may buy more song downloads because their prices are the same or less than the new price of CDs. The demand for CDs will decrease.

◀ Check the price of goods before you buy.

Economics in Action

Often, when the price of a good decreases and the good is something people need, such as tissues or napkins, people will buy more of that product at the lower price. This is referred to as buying in bulk.

▼ Food is something we need. Grocery stores offer many choices for consumers.

Prices and Quantity: The Law of Supply

As with demand, there is a connection between the price and the quantity of goods or services supplied in the market. This relationship is known as the **law of supply**.

The law of supply states that:

- as the price of goods or services rises, and other factors remain the same, the quantity produced by suppliers will increase;

- as the price of goods or services falls, and other factors remain the same, the quantity produced by suppliers will decrease.

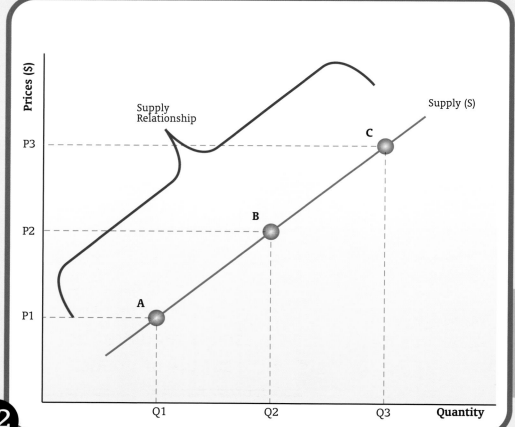

◀ This graph shows the law of supply. If the price of goods rise, quantities increase. If the price falls, quantities decrease.

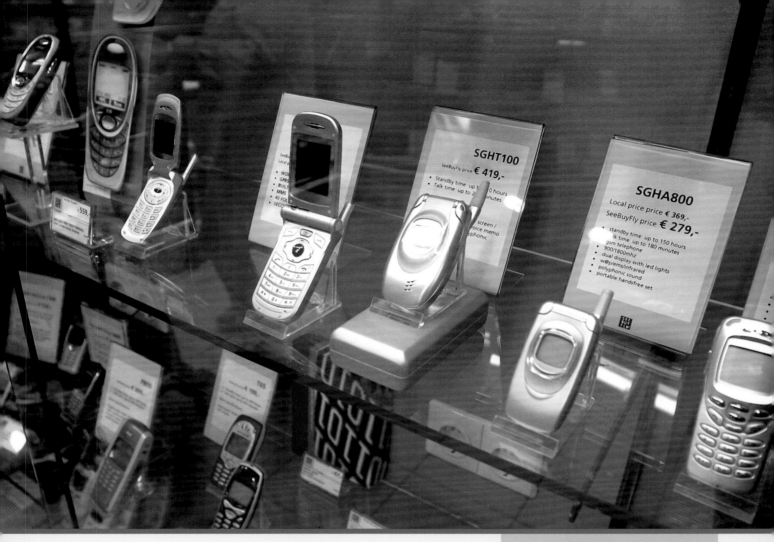

▲ Sellers offer many different kinds of cell phones to buy.

The Law of Supply and You

What does this mean? It means that if consumers are willing to buy something at a high price, the supplier will rush to make more of that item to sell, in order to increase **profits**. (A profit is when the seller makes money on what is sold.) But if consumers stop buying at that price, the supplier will stop making as many of that product.

This makes sense for the supplier. More products at higher prices means more profit. But what does it mean to you, the consumer?

Well, it means you keep paying a high price for the product—perhaps a higher price than you should!

Point of Information

Japan created a "Just in Time" process for goods. In Japan, goods are manufactured when ordered. This helps regulate the supply of goods.

Let's look at an example. You want to buy the newest cell phone. It has many more features than your current phone, but it also costs a lot more. However, many consumers feel the same way you do. They want the same phone. They don't care that it costs more than other phones. In fact, they are willing to pay even more than the current price for the phone. So manufacturers increase the price of the phone. Still, consumers think the phone is worth the new, higher price. So the manufacturer produces more phones because people will pay the higher price. The sales of the new cell phone at the higher price increase the company's profits. This is the law of supply at work.

The law of supply is also affected by time. Suppliers must react quickly to changes in price or demand. So the supplier must know why the price or demand changed. They then must quickly decide whether to increase or decrease the supply of a good or service.

◀ Climate changes can affect goods produced.

▲ Toys and products for the beach sell more in the summer when people go to beaches.

Fad or Long Term

For example, if a new style of clothing becomes popular, then suppliers must be ready to manufacture more of the item. They want to get their supply of goods into the stores while there is a demand for them. However, manufacturers have to decide if the clothing is a **fad** (a fad is an item that is popular for a short period of time) or if people will continue to buy the item for a long period of time. If suppliers think the clothing will be popular for years, then they may have to hire more workers, buy more machinery, and advertise more. These additional costs will affect the price of the clothing and may also affect the demand.

Point of Information

The law of supply is sometimes called "Say's Law" after French economist Jean Baptiste Say (1767-1832).

The Role of Competition

Prices are affected by more than just the relationship between producers and consumers, however. Manufacturers and sellers also have a big impact on price because they compete with each other for every dollar. That means they want their product to be more attractive than that of their **competitors**, and they'll do pretty much anything to make that the case—including twisting the laws of supply and demand. Let's look at the different ways suppliers do this.

▲ Sales draw consumers into stores.

Slashing Prices and Sales

Have you ever been told to wait for the sale before you buy something? Many items, such as clothing, go on sale at certain times of the year. For example, summer clothes go on sale at the end of summer so many people wait to buy their summer clothes then. Sales draw people into stores. Sometimes, stores will run a sale on just one item, while other items stay at their original price. The store hopes the sale item will lure customers in who may then buy both the sale item and other items not on sale. The sale item then becomes a so-called **loss leader**. The loss leader is a product sold at a price that is a loss for the merchant but brings in customers who also buy higher-priced items.

Other times, suppliers **slash** prices on a number of items to attract customers. This way they can sell their **inventory**, the products they have on hand, before they have to bring new products in. Car dealers often slash their prices at the end of a month or during a holiday because they have to sell their current inventory of cars before the new models arrive.

Generic versus Name Brand

Imagine that you are in a drug store. You need some cold medicine. You remember the name of a brand from an ad on TV but next to it you see a **generic brand** made by the store. It has the same ingredients and promises to do the same thing—but it's cheaper! People often buy the generic brand to save money. Which would you buy?

During tough times, people often buy more generic brands. Generic food products sell more than brand names when people have less money. Many people decide they are no longer willing to pay a higher price for a name product. Sometimes, though, people will decide that the brand name is worth the price. They may choose to buy some generic goods at a lower price so that they have enough money to buy a favorite brand of cereal or juice. Their decision is based on the quality of the brand name product. They think the brand name juice or cereal is of better quality than the generic one.

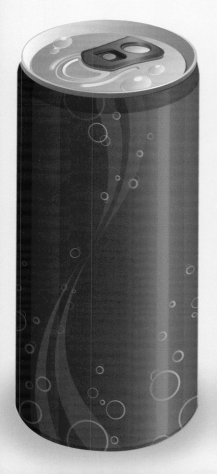

◄ People buy generic brands of soda to save money.

Substitute Products

Have you ever admired a friend's new bag and then learned that it was a cheap copy of an expensive brand? Sometimes, suppliers make copies of expensive goods. The copies are made of cheaper materials and the quality is not as good as the original, but the copies are also half the price! Are these **substitute products** worth the price or is it smarter to buy the real thing?

Another way that people substitute products is to choose something cheaper that is still something they need. Often people do this when they buy food. Say that you want to buy some meat to eat during the week. You love steak, but you see that chicken is much cheaper, so you buy the chicken. Or you may see that lamb chops are on sale, so you decide to buy the chops instead of the more expensive steak. You might even decide to buy a cheaper cut of steak. In each of these cases, you are substituting products and making choices based on price.

◀ Flea markets or thrift stores are places to find cheaper goods.

▲ People make choices about what to buy based on quality and price.

Remember, your money is a limited resource. You need to think carefully about your choices.

• Is the product of good quality?
• Are you paying a fair price for it?

Smart consumers consider whether they really need a good before purchasing it. If they decide they do, then they compare price and quality.

Economics in Action

Have you heard of the **black market**? It is when people sell goods illegally. It is called the black market because the sales often happen out of sight and sometimes in the dark!

19

Big Picture: The Global Market

You've seen what supply and demand is like on the local level. It isn't all that different on a much larger scale. Everything just gets bigger. Buyers and sellers can be multinational corporations and even entire countries. Markets can be global. For example, the market for gold is a global market. Sellers and buyers from all around the world interact with one another as they buy and sell gold.

So what happens when goods or services are provided on a global level. Which countries "demand," and which countries "supply?" That depends on a number of factors.

- **Natural Resources:** Geography—size, climate, water, minerals, fertility of soil—all determine what resources countries have. Without certain resources, countries must **import** to provide or make the goods that people need or want. On the other hand, if a country is rich in resources, it can supply, or **export**, some of them to others. For example, Canada has oil reserves, so it exports oil and petroleum to countries that need it, such as the United States. The United States imports oil. However, the United States grows a lot of wheat to export to other countries such as China and India. These countries buy wheat from the United States because they can't grow enough wheat to meet the needs of their people.

▶ Coal is a natural resource.

- **Human Resources:** People provide the labor that is necessary to produce goods. The number of people in a country, the education they receive (literacy), and the skills they have affect what goods and services can be produced. For example, some countries have many people who are trained in technology and therefore produce products in that area. The more people a country has who are trained to do different jobs, the more successful it will be. Some countries, such as Canada, have well-trained and literate people so they can produce a lot of goods and services.

▲ A strong labor force helps a country grow.

- **Capital Resources:** These are the buildings, machines, and tools needed to produce the goods. The more capital resources a country has, the more kinds of things it can produce. A country low on capital resources would have to depend on other countries to create the goods it needs. Some countries, such as Japan, have a lot of capital resources. They produce and export cars, electronics, and other products that require capital resources. Other countries, such as Ecuador, have limited capital resources. These countries have to import many manufactured goods.

▼ Capital resources are needed to make goods. These machines are used to manufacture gas.

Things Change

Supply and demand relationships can change unexpectedly. These are some ways that can change supply and demand.

Changing Values in Society

One week you drink soda every day at lunch. The next week you decide drinking soda is not healthy. You have changed your values on soda. Sometimes, many people living in a single society or culture will change how they think about a product. For example, many people today recycle, so they want containers that can be reused. That's why manufacturers now make reusable containers for coffee and other drinks instead of throwaway containers. This kind of society-wide change will dramatically increase the sale of reusable cups and other products that can be recycled.

▲ Many people now ride bikes instead of driving cars to save on gas and stop pollution.

Changes in Supply of Resources

Changes in resources can also affect the supply and demand of products. Perhaps your country mines and sells coal. Then one day the supply of coal runs out. Now your country can no longer supply the demand for coal.

War or Natural Disasters

War and natural disasters can affect goods and services. Floods may ruin crops, while war can stop the flow of goods from one region to another. War or disasters can destroy transportation systems, close down industries, and force workers to move away. Few people may be able to buy goods and services, and few workers may be able to provide them.

Technology

Advances in technology change supply and demand. Think of the advances made to phones. Phones are now like mini computers. People want their phone to have a wide array of functions. Advances in technology have affected the manufacturing, price, and applications of phones.

Number of Sellers

The growth of **chains** of stores affects supply and demand. Because these chains are large and buy huge quantities of goods, they are often able to sell them cheaper than individual stores. Sometimes, the arrival of chain stores forces local stores out of business because the chains can offer goods at lower prices.

How can an individual, company, community, or country be affected by these shifts? You've already seen the answers:

- Production increases or decreases;
- Purchasing increases or decreases;
- Quality increases or decreases;
- Price goes up or down.

Here's an example. Today, many people want to save the planet. This is a change in values. So some people drive less and look for other ways to **conserve**, or save, energy. Manufacturers produce goods that help people save energy, such as hybrid cars and new light bulbs. Saving energy means that some countries buy less oil. This change in values affects the supply and demand of oil.

Economics in Action

Do you like orange juice? Well, the price of orange juice depends on the weather. Cold weather in southern states can affect orange crops. During cold weather, fewer oranges are available to consumers. This means the price will increase. So even the weather affects supply and demand.

Finding a Balance

You've seen that price is a key factor in supply and demand. Consumers want to pay a fair price. Producers want to get a fair price for their goods that will give them a profit. But producers can't charge anything they like for their product. If the price is too high, consumers won't buy the product. The producer has to come up with a price that the consumer will pay and the market will bear.

How does the producer know when the price is right? Well, let's say the producer sells apples. There is a good quantity, and the quality is good. The producer thinks a fair price is $1.00 per apple. Other apples are selling for the same or almost the same price. The price is balanced, which means it's fair to the buyer and the market and it also gives the producer a profit. Consumers buy the producer's apples. Finding this balance has a special name in economics. It's called reaching **equilibrium**. What does that mean?

Look at the graph. It shows when the price and the quantity of goods are in equilibrium. This price has a special name: the **market clearing price (MCP)**. The MCP lets everyone benefit. Consumers find enough quantity in the marketplace, and they pay a fair price. Producers get a fair price for their goods. The price covers their costs and lets them make a profit. It's a win/win situation for all involved.

▶ This diagram show the equilibrium or market clearing price. The price is balanced.

Market Clearing Price

Surpluses and Shortages

What happens, though, when the market clearing price has not been met? What if there are too many or too few goods in the market? Well, that situation can create either a **surplus** or a **shortage** in the market.

A surplus means having extra. In supply and demand, you have a surplus when the quantity supplied is greater than the quantity demanded. Crops, such as wheat, often result in surpluses. There is more wheat for sale than is needed. Some countries, such as Canada and the United States, grow more wheat than they need, so they have surplus crops to sell. Good weather, better seeds, and advances in farming can help create surpluses.

Point of Information

Adam Smith is called the father of economics. He believed that in a free market economy prices and quantities fixed themselves to be fair to both consumers and producers. He called this idea the "invisible hand."

Shortages are the opposite of surpluses. A shortage exists when the demand is greater than the quantity supplied. Think of it this way. There were only 300 high-performance sportscars produced last year, but there was a demand for 400. Hence, there was a shortage of these sports cars. The manufacturer may have created the shortage so demand would stay high.

There are other things that can cause shortages. Sometimes, machinery breaks down. Lack of raw materials can also halt production of goods. More goods can't be produced until the machinery is fixed. Sometimes, natural disasters, such as earthquakes or floods, stop raw materials from being shipped to factories. Untrained workers can also cause shortages in manufactured goods. There can also be shortages of crops. Crop shortages are often caused by weather conditions, such as lack of rain.

▲ Droughts can cause shortages of food.

▼ The manufacturer created a shortage of sports cars so the price and demand would stay high.

Surpluses, Shortages, and You

Surpluses and shortages can affect people throughout the world. If people have too much of something, they can use that product to build their wealth. For example, the Middle East has a surplus of oil. Most of the people in the world need oil. They use it to heat their homes, drive their cars, and manufacture goods. Because the people in the Middle East control the supply of oil, they gain power over the people in other nations that need oil. Variations in the supply and demand of oil can affect you and your family. If the demand for oil is high, the price will probably be high, and your family may have to conserve oil. If the demand for oil is low, then the price will be low, too, and you and your family will be able to use oil more freely.

Shortages can cause people great hardship, especially if there is a shortage in supplies for basic needs. For example, there may be a shortage of food because the summer is dry and the crops have failed. Usually, other countries will have a surplus of food, which they can ship to the people who need it.

Shortages may cause you to have to do without certain goods, too. However, most shortages are annoying but not critically important. You may be surprised by an unexpected shortage of your favorite snack food at your local food store, but you find plenty of options. So you just choose something else.

▲ The Middle East has some of the largest oil reserves in the world.

Economics and YOU

Scalpers sell event tickets at prices much higher than what the ticket office charges. They are successful when there is a shortage of tickets to an event. People will then pay high prices for tickets. Some scalpers actually help create this shortage. Can you guess how? They buy up the best seats!

The Government Steps In

In a free market economy, the MCP often adjusts itself. Prices, supply, and demand go up and down naturally. There are times, however, when prices, supply, and demand of certain goods need help. Reasons might include protecting consumers or producers. At those times, the government steps in to control prices in the market. They do this by enforcing **price ceilings** and **price floors**. What are they? Let's look at each one.

Think of the key word: ceiling. A ceiling is high up. It's at the top. So a price ceiling is the top price. A price ceiling sets the **maximum**, or highest, price that consumers will pay. Often, price ceilings are set for certain goods (oil), wages (executive pay), rent (rent control), and interest rates. These goods or services are usually things people need.

For example, oil is a resource people need to heat their homes, run their cars, and use in manufacturing. Therefore, they will always have to buy oil in the near future. So the government sets a price ceiling on oil. This way, people will always be able to afford oil.

▼ Sometimes governments step in to protect consumers.

Now let's look at a price floor. A floor is at the bottom. So a price floor is the **minimum**, or lowest, price for which a good or service can be sold. A price floor often applies to agriculture (wheat) or wages (minimum wage). This means if the price floor for wheat is $2.00 a bushel, then that is the lowest price at which it can be sold. Wages work the same way. Imagine that you are working at a local store. You can't be paid less than the minimum wage. As of July 2009, the minimum wage set by the federal government is $7.25 per hour. Some states have set a minimum wage that is even higher than that.

Governments collect information about supply and demand and markets. This information helps governments make decisions about when to set price ceilings or floors.

▲ Teens often earn minimum wage in their first jobs.

Economics in Action

The European Union changed its **subsidies** to farmers so that now payment is made to farmers for using production practices that protect the environment and promote food safety. The farmers receive subsidies to encourage them to keep the environment safe.

Remember: It's About You

The government may sometimes step in to help consumers, but in the end it's all about you. Remember, your money is a limited resource. Think about whether ads are making you want something you don't really need. Ask yourself if a price is fair, or is the item expensive because of high demand. Don't confuse a high price with quality. Remember the laws of supply and demand. These actions will make you a smart shopper!

Glossary

advertising Promotes a particular product by describing its benefits and creating a perceived need; how suppliers influence people's choices of what to buy

black market When people sell goods illegally

capital resources The buildings, machines, and tools needed to produce goods

chain A series of things connected or related to each other

competitor A person or business that tries to win or gain something from others

conserve To save

consumer A person who buys and uses up things

demand The number of consumers willing and able to purchase a good or service at a given price

economy How a country manages its money, goods and services, and resources

equilibrium Balance

export Something that is sold or traded to another country

fad Something that is very popular for a short time

free market economy When a country buys and sells things without interference from outside sources

generic brand A product that does the same thing as a trademarked product but costs less

goods Any object a person wants or needs to help them survive

human resources The knowledge and skills that workers have

hybrid Combining two methods of fueling a car to make the car more efficient

import Something that is brought in from another country for sale or use

intangible Something that is experienced rather than owned

inventory The products a supplier has on hand

law of demand If the price of goods goes up, people buy less of it, if all other things are equal; if the price of goods goes down, people buy more of it, if all other things are equal

law of supply As the price of goods or services rises, and other factors remain the same, the quantity produced by suppliers will increase; as the price of goods or services falls, and other factors remain the same, the quantity produced by suppliers will decrease

loss leader A product sold at a price that is a loss for the merchant but brings in customers who also buy higher-priced items

manufacture To make or process something, especially in quantity and with the use of machinery

market clearing price (MCP) When consumers find enough quantity in the marketplace and pay a fair price while producers get a fair price that covers their costs and gives them a profit

maximum The greatest possible number or amount

minimum The smallest or least possible amount

natural resources Materials that occur naturally in the earth, such as minerals, water, trees, and land

price ceiling Setting a maximum, or the highest, price that consumers pay

price floor The minimum, or lowest, price that a good or service can be sold for

profit The amount of money left after all the costs of running a business have been paid

quantity A number or amount

services Actions or activities one person performs for another

shortage When the demand is greater than the quantity supplied

slash When merchants cut their prices sharply to attract customers

subsidy Financial aid given by one person or government to another

substitute products Copies of expensive goods; usually made of cheaper materials and not as well made as the original

supply The quantity of resources, goods, or services that sellers offer at various prices at a particular time

surplus When the quantity supplied is greater than the quantity demanded

Index

advertising 9, 15, 17

black market 19
Brazil 7

Canada 7, 20, 21, 25
capital resources 21
chain stores 23
China 7, 20
competition 16

disasters 22, 26

Ecuador 21
equilibrium 24
European Union 29
exports 20, 21

fads 15
free market economy 7

generic brand 17
global markets 20
government 7, 28, 29

human resources 21

imports 20
India 20
inventory 17

Japan 7, 21

law of demand 10, 11
law of supply 12–15
loss leader 16

market clearing price (MCP) 24, 25, 28
Mexico 7
minimum wage 29

natural resources 20

price ceiling 28, 29
price floor 28, 29
profit 13, 14, 24

Russia 7

sales 16
Say, Jean Baptiste 15
scalper 27
shortage 25, 26
Smith, Adam 25
subsidy 29
substitute products 18
surplus 24, 25, 26, 27

technology 21, 23

United States 6, 7, 20, 25

values 22, 23

Webfinder

www.piggybank.co.uk
http://realtrees4kids.org/ninetwelve/supply.htm
www.econedlink.org
www.socialstudiesforkids.com